SOUTHPORT
THROUGH TIME
Jack Smith

AMBERLEY

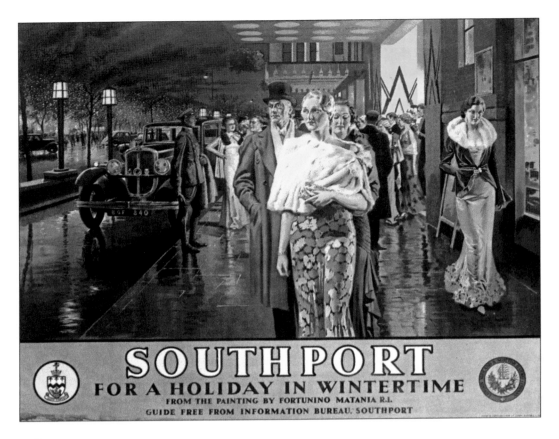

Railway Poster

Since Southport became a popular resort to visit, it was always regarded as being rather affluent and upmarket. The town was served by no less than three railway stations from the later 1890s, which brought holidaymakers and daytrippers from near and far. Here we see a typical railway poster from around the 1920s, painted by Fortunino Matania who was commissioned to do a poster series for Southport. The illustration shows elegant ladies and gentlemen leaving the Scarisbrick Hotel on Lord Street after a function. Note the uniformed chauffeur.

First published 2012

Amberley Publishing
The Hill, Stroud
Gloucestershire, GL5 4EP

www.amberley-books.com

Copyright © Jack Smith, 2012

The right of Jack Smith to be identified as the Author of this work has been asserted in accordance with the Copyrights, Designs and Patents Act 1988.

ISBN 978 1 4456 0275 2

British Library Cataloguing in Publication Data.
A catalogue record for this book is available from the British Library.

Typeset in 9.5pt on 12pt Celeste.
Typesetting by Amberley Publishing.
Printed in the UK.

Introduction

Southport did not exist at the end of the eighteenth century, but there was a beach with sandhills and a few fishermen's dwellings were located here. A man who realised that the beach might attract visitors was the landlord of the Black Bull in Churchtown, a small village two miles from the seashore. He saw future potential here; his name was William (Duke) Sutton.

He started taking visitors from his hotel, by horse and carriage, through two miles of sand dunes to the beach. These visits were advertised and word spread so that they became a profitable sideline for the Churchtown landlord. The popularity of the seaside visits led to Sutton building changing rooms in a wooden shack in 1792. The building was ridiculed by many, who said his venture would come to nought and his building was a 'folly'. 'Duke's Folly' was the first building in what was then an un-named place in North Meols. By 1798, the shack was superseded by a small, brick hotel, known as Original Hotel or South Port Hotel. At the hotel opening, it is alleged, the name 'South Port' was given to the area.

From the early 1800s the popularity of the area grew due to improved public transport, particularly the Lancaster Canal to Scarisbrick. By 1849 Lord Street was developed on both sides, but the area was still surrounded by sand hills. A short seawall had been built, but the street occasionally flooded. The railway arrived in 1848, boosting further development of houses and hotels, including the Victoria on the promenade. However, there was a lack of attractions for the increasing number of visitors!

A baths was built and bathing machines were sited by the shore for public use. In 1860 a pier was constructed, originally 1,200 yards long and lengthened by a jetty in 1868 to 1,400 yards. Here steamers moored, plying between Barrow, Blackpool and Llandudno. Things were looking up for the town, now called 'Southport', especially as a new Winter Gardens complex had been opened in 1874. By the 1880s, many family run businesses and shops had been established. The seafront promenade saw more hotels built, such as the Royal Hotel, today's Royal Clifton. The licence for this hotel was originally that granted to Sutton's Original Hotel.

A major problem came to light during the 1880s. The sea was retreating from the foreshore! The retraction of the sea proved to be of benefit to the Cheshire Lines Railway in building its line from Ainsdale to Southport, as it allowed a curved embankment to be constructed across the former beach to create a terminus in Lord Street in 1884. The 1880s and '90s saw the building of the two marine lakes and further seafront development. Also, horse-drawn, and later electric, trams improved transport around the town.

The twentieth century saw Southport on a low, but becoming a high status area by the end of it. The sea's retraction from the north seafront allowed a large area to be reclaimed; golf links, housing and limited industry are now to be found here. The foreshore and parks have now partially given way to the North and South Ocean Plaza complex, and a new Pleasureland has opened. The marine lake (north) was widened and extended in the 1960s.

Among the 'lows' has been the ill-fated Winter Gardens scheme in the 1990s, whereby the former Cheshire line's railway station and the old Winter Gardens site were to be developed over 11 acres, a project which started and stopped over the years. The railway station had closed in 1952, becoming a bus station until 1987, then being abandoned for some years. In 1993 Safeway supermarket acquired the site and built a store on part of the land scheduled for development; the store is now Morrisons. The Floral Hall gained a theatre, but sadly lost its gardens, replaced by a hotel!

The 'highs' saw a new pier and suspension bridge on Marine Way. Shops and hotels changed their frontage in/around Lord Street, and the Town Hall and civic gardens were refurbished and upgraded. These past two years we have had no library or art gallery due to refurbishment work.

The sea still retreats, but this will allow more exciting foreshore development after reclamation. Soon there will be the refurbishment of the whole of Kings Garden and its environs around the marine lake. This will see the gardens and pavilions all restored to landscape architect Mawson's designs of 1911. The photographs to follow can provide only a glimpse of *Southport Through Time*.

Jack Smith
July 2012

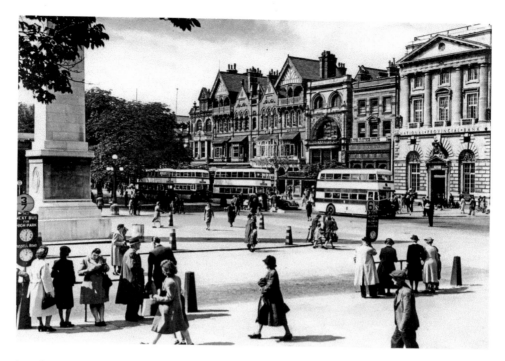

London Square

Although a similar view to that on the opposite page, here we look across from the east side of Lord Street to the buildings previously described. However we now incorporate the base of Southport's war memorial obelisk to the left of the picture. The older view here also shows the present Waterstone's building with its bank name across the front, as it was in the 1940s and '50s. It is also of interest to note that Martins Bank is telling people to 'Buy Defence Bonds'. The clothes that people are wearing are a clue to the date of the photograph. There will be more on London Square later when we look at the east side of Lord Street.

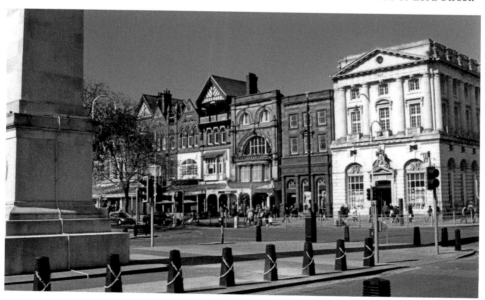

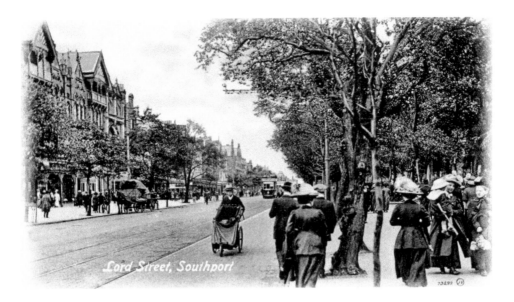

Lord Street, Southport

The Albany Building

This large building adjoins the terracotta-fronted building, and is three down from Waterstone's. This is the remarkable building with mock-Elizabethan timber-framed gables; the front-facing gables contain verandas. Compared to the previous picture, here we can more easily see the four roof pitches of the individual shops that were incorporated when the building was erected in 1884. The four shopkeepers were Mr Adams (chemist), Mr Evans (tailor), Mr Robson (ironmonger), and Mr Witham (wine merchant). It was Mr Witham, whose business had started in 1860, who erected the building. The right-hand end shop, owned originally by Mr Witham, houses Barclays Bank in this old photograph. In today's photograph, note the classical exterior of the former Preston Bank building to the extreme left (HSBC today), and see inset.

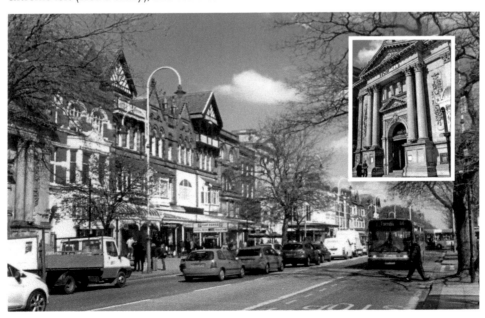

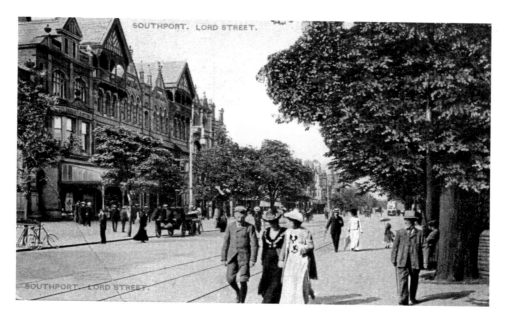

SOUTHPORT. LORD STREET.

SOUTHPORT LORD STREET.

Traffic Changes

Again we look at the Albany Building, this time looking in the northern direction across the front of it. The view dates from about 1912. To the right of centre in the distance is a tram, the rails being clearly visible in the roadway. In 1870 the Tramways Act was passed, following the upsurge of interest in the construction of tram systems in towns throughout the country. By 1871, the population of Southport had reached 21,000, and it was felt to be the right time for a tram system to be constructed, the town being served only by horse-drawn carriages at this time. A tramway company was formed in May 1871, and a route built between Birkdale and Churchtown. The tramways are now long gone and buses cover routes into and around the town. Park & Ride facilities exist for visitors.

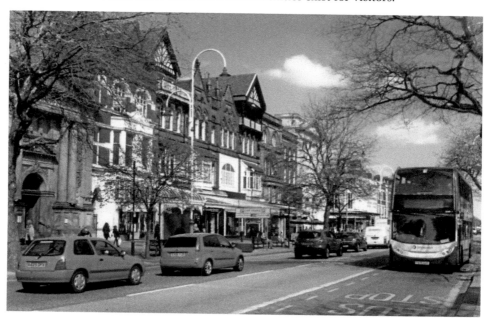

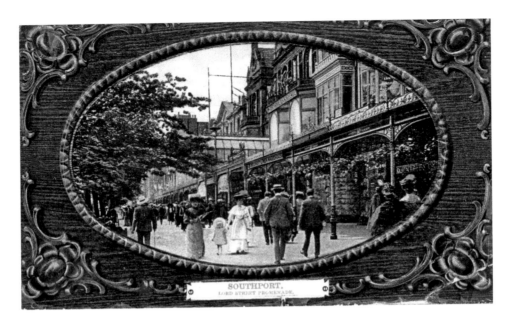

SOUTHPORT.
LORD STREET PROMENADE.

Wayfarer's Arcade

In our old view we look along the canopies that are so typical of Lord Street's shop frontages towards the entrance archway to the Wayfarer's Arcade (originally called Leyland Arcade). The postcard is dated 'Southport 1909' (written in pencil to a Northampton address). The view will predate this of course. The clothes worn by the people in the old and new pictures provide interesting comparisons. The arcade accommodates shops on each side of the entrance passageway, which opens out to form a sitting area used for music performances and café customers. A high, arched roof of iron and glass covers the sitting area. There are also shops on the upstairs galleries. The whole of the arcade was restored to its original splendour in 1981. Today's view of the arcade entrance shows hardly any changes.

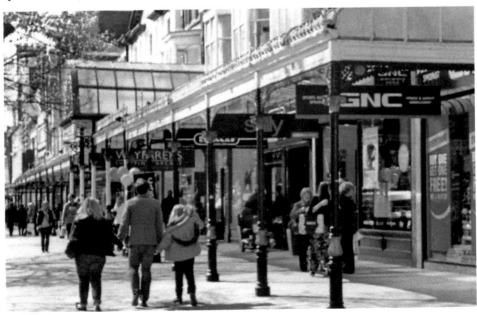

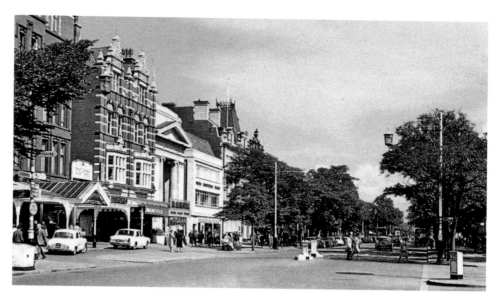

The Scarisbrick Hotel

The present hotel was built in 1881, where the former Scarisbrick Arms used to stand. That establishment was set up by one Thomas Mawdesley in the 1820s and originally named the Hesketh Arms. The present hotel had an additional storey added after a fire in 1945. The architecture of the hotel is striking, but only really noticeable from across the street where both our views were taken. The hotel has some sixty rooms and is one of the town's more popular places to stay. It was the entrance to this hotel that the artist Fortunino Matania chose for his painting depicting Southport scenes, used as a poster by the Cheshire Lines Railway (see page 2). Next door to the hotel is yet another striking example of Lord Street's multi-period architecture. Another building with classical columned exterior, it was originally the National Westminster Bank.

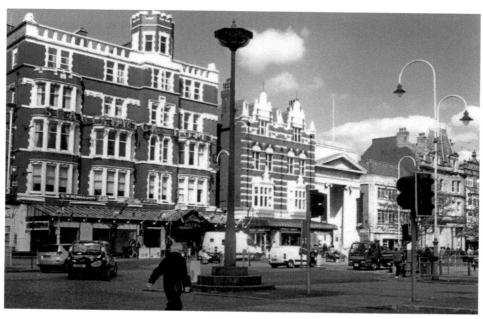

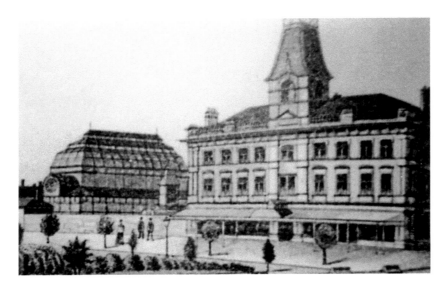

The Pavilion Building

The Pavilion Building in the 2012 picture was built adjacent to the site once occupied by the Winter Gardens complex. The Winter Gardens buildings, to the left in the sepia view, were built in 1874 and started with a company holding £30,000. The project occupied land from Lord Street to what was the promenade at that time, the sea receding some distance from the promenade, even at high tide. The end 'wings' of the building accommodated a conservatory with space for meetings etc. (bigger than the Palm House at Kew), and a pavilion with concert hall accommodating audiences of 2,000. The two ends were joined by a covered 'promenade' walkway, 170 feet long, facing the sea. It was believed to be one of the biggest buildings erected on an English seafront. It is thought that the modern building is so-called to commemorate the former Winter Gardens Pavilion that was close by.

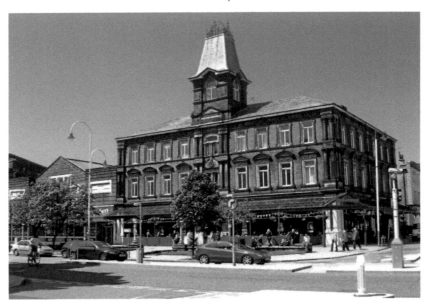

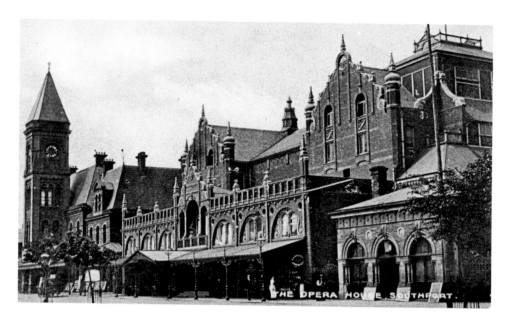

The Opera House

By the 1890s the south end of the Winter Garden building, formerly the Conservatory, was converted into a ballroom and roller-skating rink, while the Pavilion Concert Hall end of the building was turned into a cinema, to resolve the lack of live artists and to enhance the appeal of the whole complex. A new opera house was built close to the Winter Garden Pavilion. The architect was Frank Matcham. It was opened in September 1891 and hosted many famous entertainers of the time. In 1929, a disastrous fire destroyed the building. In 1930, and rising from the foundations of the former Opera House, a new theatre was built – the Garrick. It played host to many stars, including George Formby and Tommy Handley. Today the building accommodates a Bingo Hall.

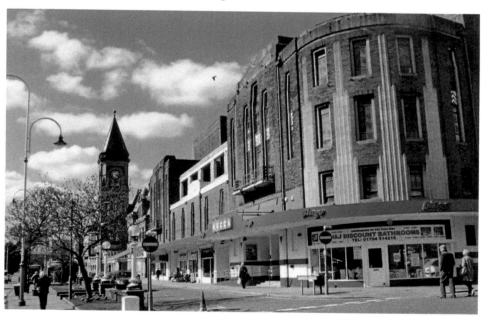

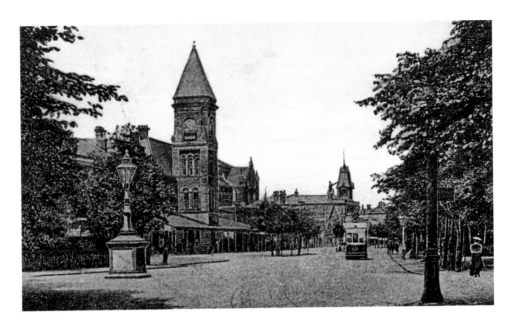

Lord Street Railway Station

The frontage of this former railway station was built as the 'Ribble Buildings', complete with tower, in 1882/83, and opened as the Southport and Cheshire lines extension railway station in 1884. The construction of the line was rather a gamble at the time, for its route out of the station to the south-west took the curving line over the beach, where an embankment was built, for by now the sea was retreating and reclamation of land was under consideration. This new station provided another route for passengers to travel to Southport, now growing in popularity with daytrippers. At this time there were other stations in the town. Both our views look north up Lord Street with the railway station to the left, and a tram in the distance to the right (see following page also). Lord Street Station closed in 1952.

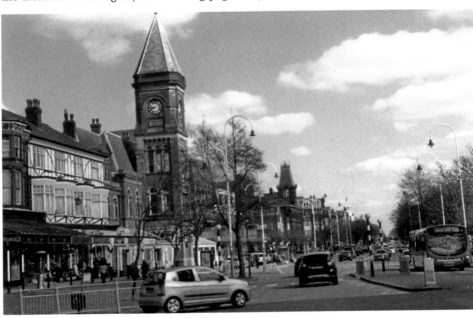

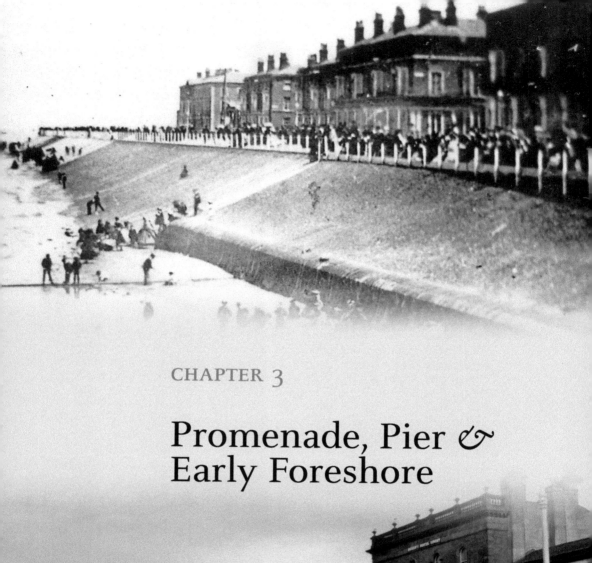

CHAPTER 3

Promenade, Pier & Early Foreshore

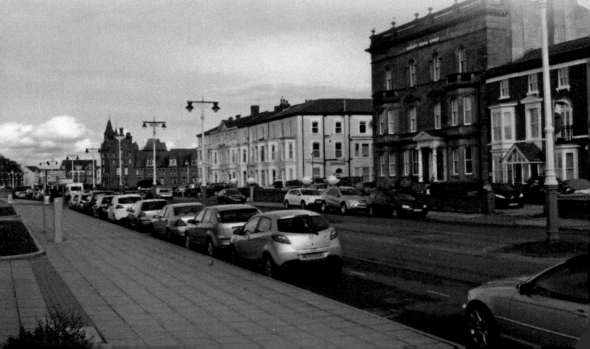

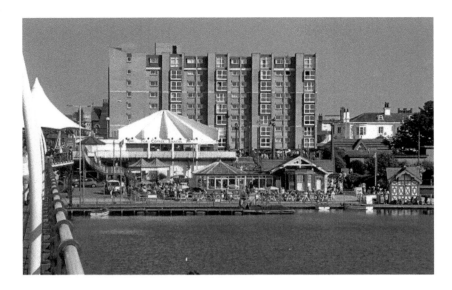

The Victoria Hotel

From the 1790s to the 1830s, a village in North Meols was called South Port. It was Southport from 1834, when development had taken place along Lord Street. Development across the sand dunes allowed the first seawall to be built from 1839, to create a promenade. The 1840s and '50s saw more development along the promenade. The foreshore was purchased for the town in 1885. The Victoria Hotel opened in 1842. It was built by John Salter, owner for twenty years, at the promenade junction with Nevill Street. The hotel was greatly extended during its life, but was demolished in the 1970s to be replaced by a multi-storey apartment block! The sepia view shows the Victoria Hotel right of centre, with the Victoria Baths to the left, in around 1850. The 2012 view shows the replacement apartment block of the 1970s, as viewed from the pier. Note the Nevill Street subway to the beach in the old image.

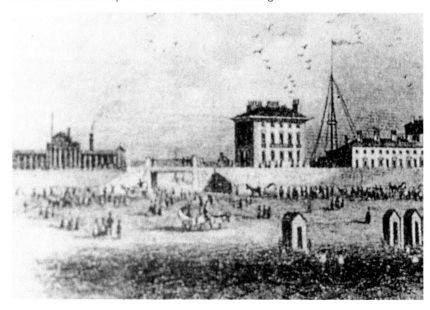

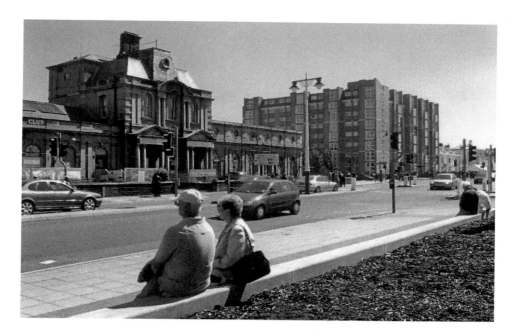

The Early Promenade

In our old view here we see a painting by E. Vernon, dated 1850, of the early promenade. The Victoria Baths building is to the left, and the Victoria Hotel to the right of it across Nevill Street, which at this time extended to the beach via a subway under the promenade; its exit is visible in the seawall. The baths and the cottages beyond the hotel are visible in the painting, as they are today. To the right on the seawall is a building called the 'promenade lodge', a shop built by one Samuel Whitely in around 1840. The sea is depicted with waves striking the seawall at a point just about where the people are sitting in the 2012 photograph! It is hard to believe that the sea has retracted so much over the past 170 years, and is about ½ mile away now.

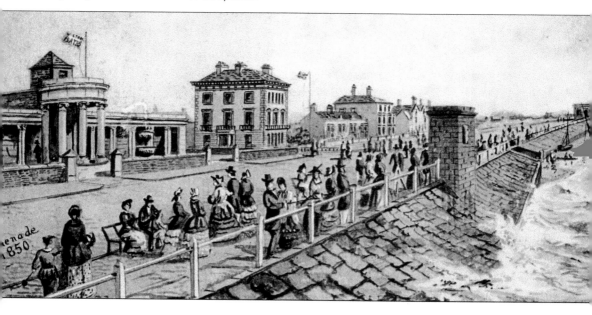

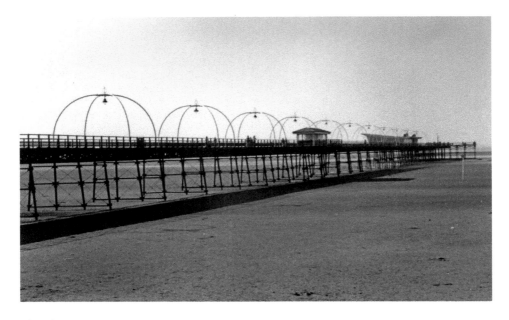

The Pier

Work commenced on a pier in Southport in 1859. It opened to the public in 1860, claiming to be the country's first 'iron pier'. Originally 1,200 yards long, its extension to 1,465 yards in 1868 made it the longest pier in the country. From the pier, steamers sailed to Blackpool, Barrow, the Isle of Man, and Llandudno. They stopped in the 1920s due to silting up of the channel. Another pierhead attraction, the divers were men who dived from pier to sea, sometimes on bicycles, such as 'Professors' Powsey, Osborne, Pearson and Sydney Smith are often mentioned. There was entertainment at the end of the pier by Blanche Laughton's orchestra, until fire destroyed their venue in 1933 after fourteen seasons of them playing there. Our old view is from a postcard of 1914 and shows the pier with steamer mooring extension. Today's rebuilt pier, albeit to its shorter length, usually shows more beach than sea beneath it.

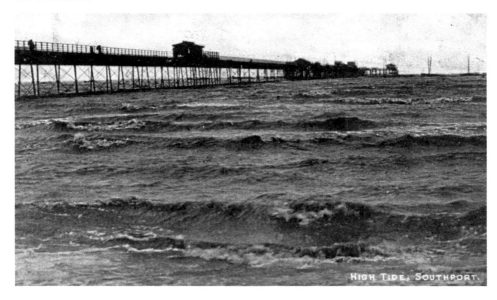

HIGH TIDE, SOUTHPORT.

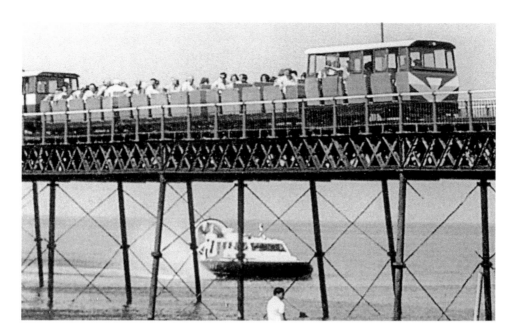

Approaching the Pierhead

Walking from the promenade to the end of Southport pier is a good 'constitutional', for it is some 1,200 yards or so! Or one may travel by tram, the only one in Southport nowadays. For about one third of the distance, the pier crosses the marine lake, Prince's Park and the South Ocean Plaza development as far as the beach, then continues over the sands to the pierhead, from which steamer trips were available until the 1920s. The 1930s saw a café and small theatre there. Our sepia picture shows the pier 'railway' with hovercraft about to depart for Blackpool Beach in around the 1970s. The hovercraft service ran from 1973 into the 1990s. Clearance for the service to recommence after trials was given in 2005, but sadly it did not resume. The hovercraft revisited the sands at the 2009 air show. The 2012 picture shows the pier tram en route to the distant pierhead.

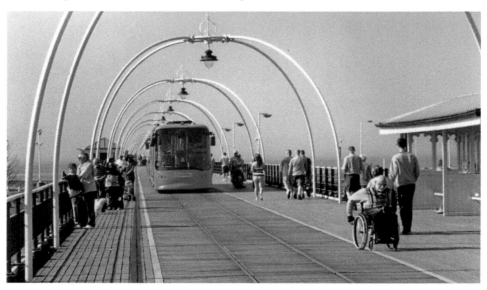

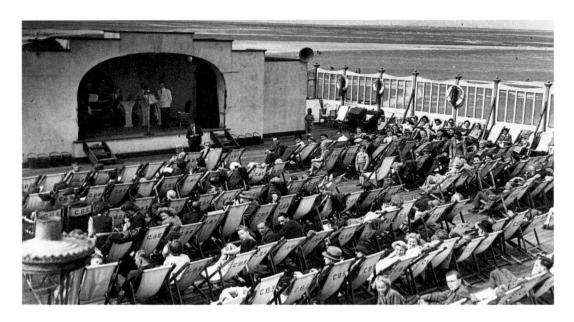

At the End of the Pier

In the post-war years the pierhead underwent a refurbishment of attractions in the form of amusement arcade, café and the essential ice cream and 'Southport rock' vendors' stalls etc. The 1950s saw an open-air theatre in use, surrounded by panels to keep the winds away, it must certainly have been a 'bracing' experience to sit in such an auditorium, as shown in our photograph from the mid-1950s. The photograph looking across the River Ribble estuary includes Blackpool Tower, in the distance above the middle lifebelt. Today the end of the pier has no such entertainment other than a café and an interesting arcade of 1950s slot machines where you use the old coinage. Looking toward Blackpool from pierhead, the open area now looks like the deck of a ship and is a great place to get one's fill of 'fresh air' in 2012.

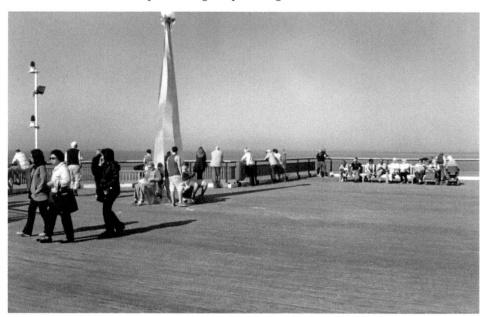

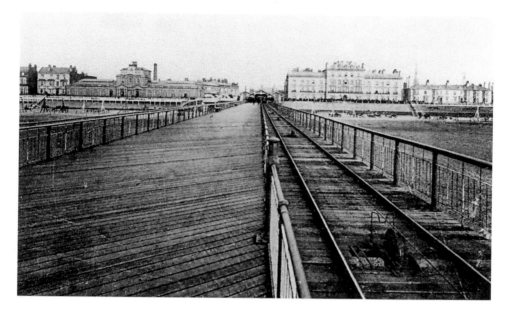

Return To Promenade

This late 1880s view is from approximately where today's skateboard area is located between Marine Drive and the pier, where the Mary Willet day nursery used to be. It tells us much about the pier and environs of the time: the pier entrance buildings are almost non-existent. The pier train was hauled by a cable (to the right), and the subway from Nevill Street to the beach was in use. The Victoria Hotel, with side extensions, was standing. The north marine lake had not yet been built (it was completed in 1892), and there was a 'beach' between the south marine lake and the promenade. Today's photograph, taken in May 2012, also looks toward the promenade. The baths are in both photographs, to the left, but the Victoria Hotel has been replaced. Marine Way, with its new bridgeis to the left of today's image..

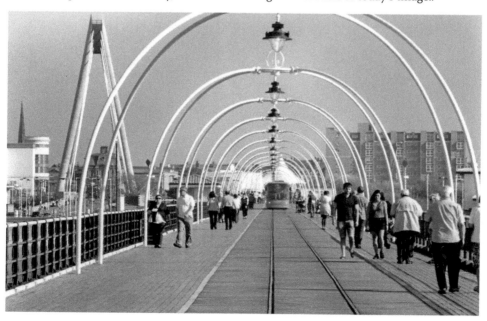

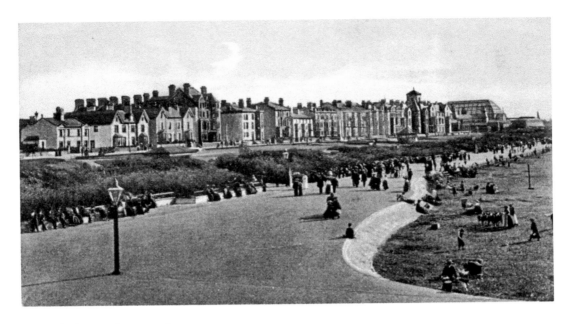

The Lower Promenade

Following the construction of the south marine lake by 1887, a section of 'beach' was created to the east side of the lake. Adjoining these 'sands' was a wide walkway running parallel to the promenade with gardens between them. This was the Lower promenade. The old view shows the 'sands', which were in fact on the edge of the marine lake, not the sea. On the beach, donkey rides are available. In the distance the Winter Gardens Palm House is visible to the right. Today's view is also taken from the pier, almost in the same place as the old view. Just above the centre of the picture, the former Lower promenade is still there. Now this area is part of Kings Gardens, and a crazy golf course is where the beach used to be. The edge of the south marine lake is to the bottom right of today's view.

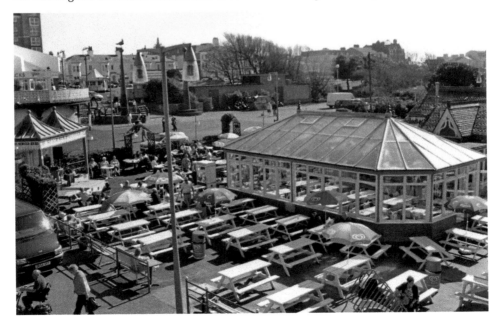

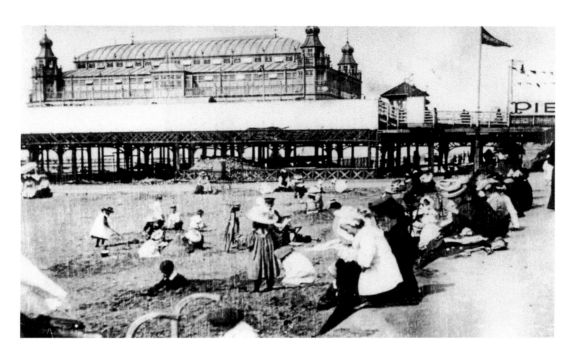

The Pier from the Old Beach

In this old photograph we look back towards the pier pavilion from the lower promenade, as featured opposite this page. The pavilion replaced an earlier one that burned down in 1897. This one was completed in 1902, indicating that the image was taken around 1902/03. The new pavilion had seating for 1,200 persons, and was a popular venue for the increasing number of visitors to Southport. The children here are doing what they do today, just enjoying the sands. But note their dress! There were no shorts then, and hats had to be worn. Today's view is rather bland and without merit in composition, but it was taken with the comparison in mind, not for its aesthetic interest! Personally, I feel that a pier theatre should have been retained instead of the amusement arcade of today.

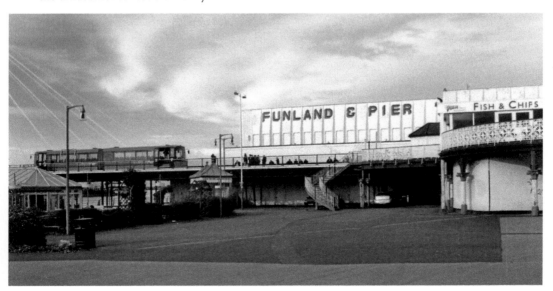

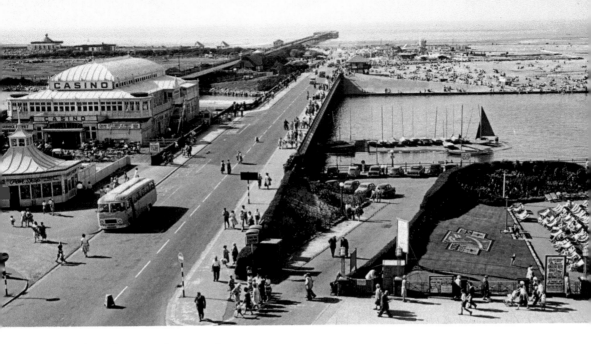

Marine Way From Promenade

The sepia view was taken probably in 1961, from a high position that I am unable to replicate today. It is a view from which, with a magnifying glass, much information can be gleaned. Marine Way is in the centre, with the pier alongside. To the right is the Floral Hall, with an advertisement for the 1962 Southport Flower Show. Another poster tells us there is dancing to the Edwin Harper Orchestra in the Floral Hall, while at the Casino 'Let's Have a Party' is hosted by Harry Hudson. To the right is the family or children's beach with 'Peter Pan's Playground' beyond. Note also the circular open-air bathing pool to the left. Today's view from ground level shows the new Marine Way Bridge and part of the pier frontage from the end of Nevill Street.

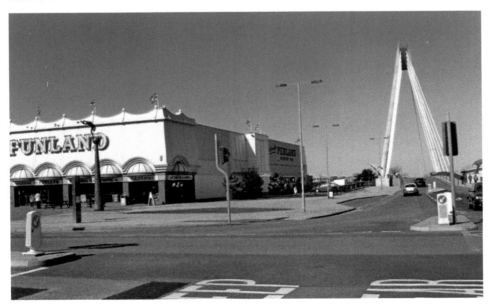

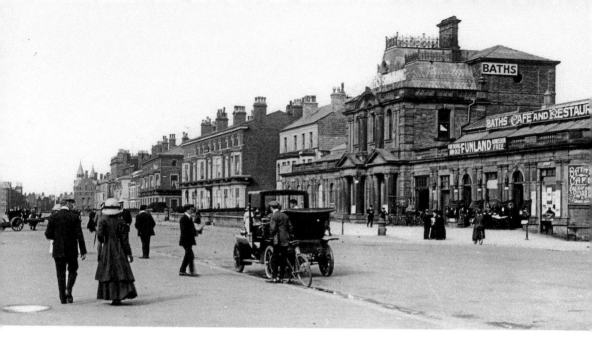

The Victoria Baths

At the junction of Nevill Street with the promenade stands the Victoria Baths. The present building dates from 1871, replacing the previous baths building that was erected in 1838 at a cost then of £6,000. The new baths had separate entrances, swimming pools, seven plunge pools and sixty-nine private baths divided into first, second and third class. Swimming lessons and displays by accomplished swimmers were held regularly. Adjoining the baths on Nevill Street was a 'large and commodious café' opened in 1888, which could accommodate almost 300 persons. The new baths was built in the 'Italian and Grecian styles' by Horton & Bridgford of Manchester at a cost of £40,000. Our early 1900s sepia view shows the baths' frontage to the promenade (note the building with pointed roof features to the left), while our present-day view provides an interesting comparison of how the building and its functions have changed.

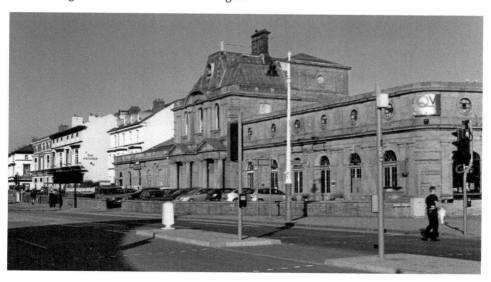

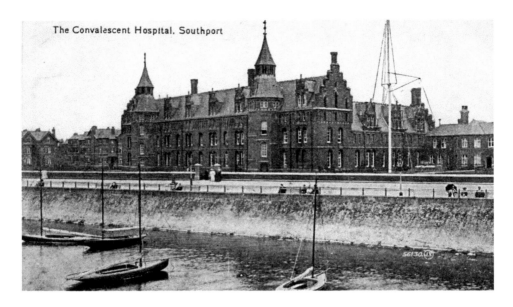

The Convalescent Hospital, Southport

The Convalescent Hospital

The promenade Convalescent Hospital is at the northern end of the promenade, opposite the north marine lake, where the founding 'Strangers Charity' established it in 1806. The site has two buildings within its bounds. The larger building, with its huge architectural and aesthetic appeal, was completed in 1852, but has subsequent extensions to sides and rear in the same French Château architectural style as the original. Up to 1948 it was a Voluntary Hospital, until it became part of the NHS that year. It was used as a military hospital in both World Wars. In 1988/90 the hospital closed, due to the opening of the new Southport Hospital, which was opened by Princess Diana. It remained unused until the later 1990s, when an application for its conversion to apartments was approved and work began. Both views show the Grade Two listed building frontage in the 1900s and in 2012, now called 'Marine Gate Mansions'.

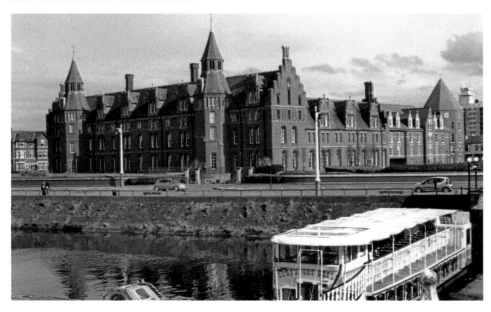

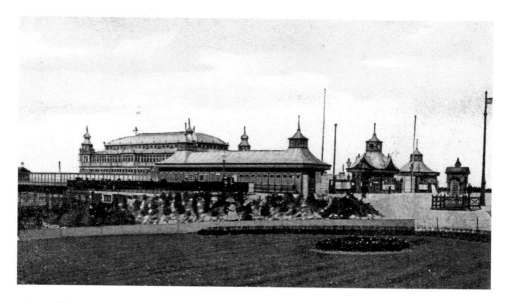

Pier Buildings and South Promenade

Returning back along the promenade past the north marine lake, we pass the Marine Drive (now renamed Marine Way), built in 1894, and pier entrance. The old view dates from about 1912, and shows the pier entrance buildings to the right, with three conical roofs. Beyond is the pier pavilion, rebuilt in 1902 with its corner minarets. To the extreme right-hand side is the Fearnley drinking fountain, which was originally sited close to the pier entrance. John Fearnley was born in 1796 and became a wealthy industrialist. He came to Southport in the 1850s and funded the building of churches and an infirmary, and the purchase of a lifeboat named *Eliza Fearnley*, lost with the crew in the 1886 *Mexico* disaster. The modern view shows the pier buildings to the left, a 'gallopers' roundabout with awning above and to the right the frontage of the new Ramada Hotel.

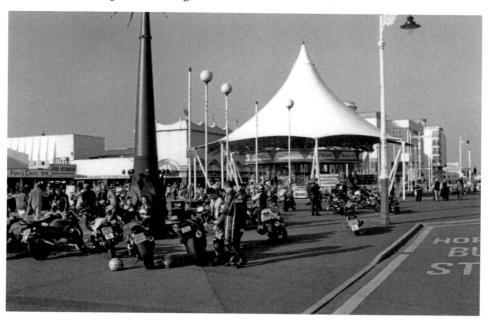

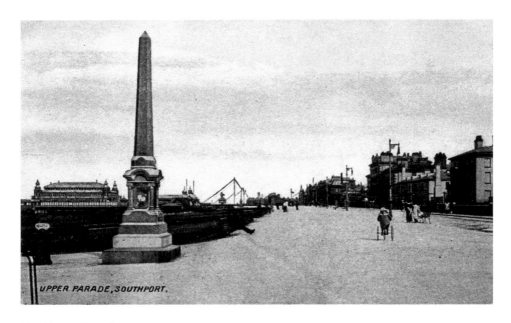

UPPER PARADE, SOUTHPORT.

The Upper Parade

Again we look back to the pier frontage in this view from the 1900s. To the left are gardens, called Kings Gardens from 1913, following their opening by King George V. The gardens were under construction from 1910 to the 1930s and were built to Thomas Mawson's design. The wide footpath was called Upper Parade. (Lower Parade was by the marine lake.) The south side of the pier pavilion is visible. To the right is the Victoria Hotel. The obelisk to the left is a memorial bearing the names of boats lost over the years off Southport's shore. It has the following poignant inscription: '*Will some kind hand please place a flower on this obelisk, in honour of all lifeboatmen*'. The main memorial to the lifeboatmen lost in the *Mexico* disaster in 1886 is in Duke Street Cemetery. The new Marine Way Bridge over the lake is visible; its tall columns and support cables are to the extreme left.

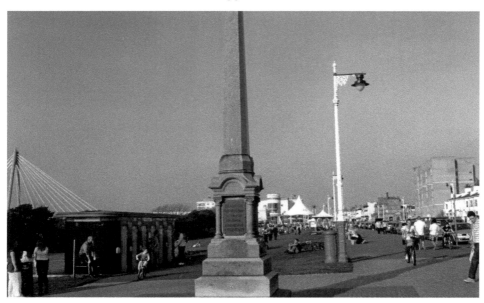

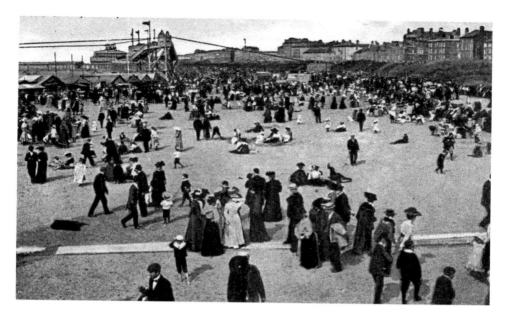

A Funfair Established

By the early 1900s it was time to give the increasing number of visitors more to see and do in Southport – then tell people at home by postcard! The funfair was established from 1903 onwards, on land stretching from the east side of the marine lake to the south end. This old view is from a postcard dated July 1905. The first amusement was a water chute, built by 1904, with the 'Maxim Flying Machine' ride almost complete. By 1908 an 'aerial ride', by cableway carried people over the marine lake, from towers each side (closed in 1911). By 1913 the funfair comprised river caves, a helter-skelter, a rollercoaster, a figure of eight ride, a wall of death, a pierrot show and stalls and sideshows. The 2012 view looks at the same location.

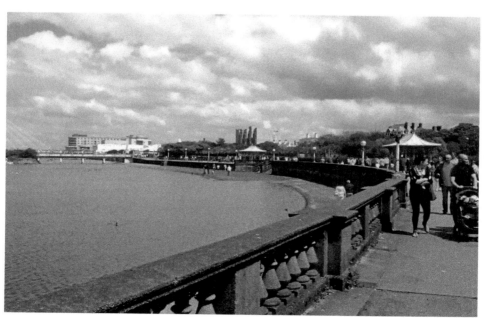

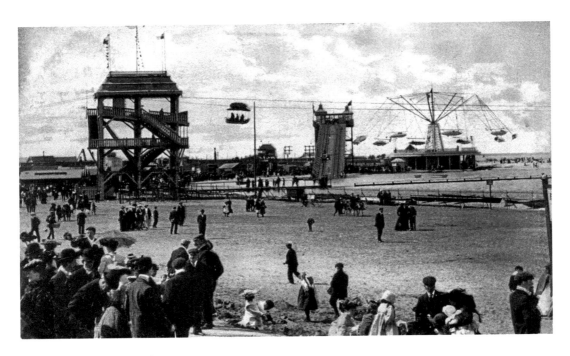

South Marine Lake Sands

Looking from the south east corner of the marine lake northwards, we see the 'sands' replicating the seashore: a busy scene with visitors to the fairground. The aerial cableway ride over the marine lake is in use. The image is from a hand-coloured postcard, unfortunately unused, so the date is a little vague, but the funfair was here from 1887 to 1923. When we look at views such as this, showing the types of clothes worn at the time, do we all wonder why 'sports clothes' were never a consideration? We always see suited gents and long-skirted ladies, all wearing hats. As for children's 'seaside clothing', that too was non-existent! In the modern photograph the curve of the lake suggests that both views were from near this spot.

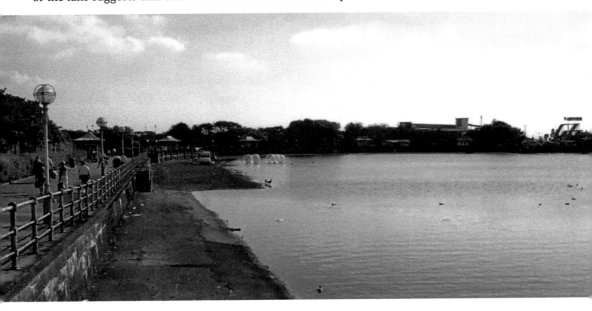

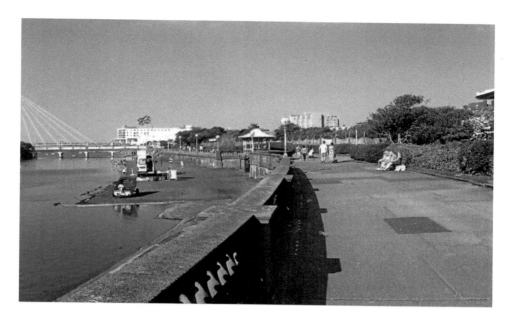

Kings Gardens, South Lake

The former location of the fairground at the south east corner of the marine lake was here between 1887 and 1923. We can see the changes that had taken place after the Marine Gardens officially became the Kings Gardens, following their official opening by King George V and Queen Mary in 1913. The water chute and flying machines and all the other sideshows and stalls have now been re-located to Pleasureland. The area where the funfair was, at this south end of the lake, is still gardens. Note that the original seawall was along the promenade from the upper left to right, before the sea began to recede. The April 2012 image was taken at ground level from the curving balustrade wall and pathway, in about the same location.

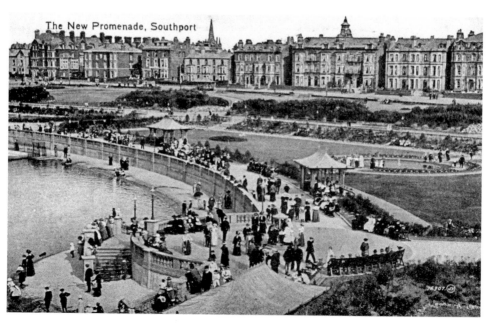

The New Promenade, Southport

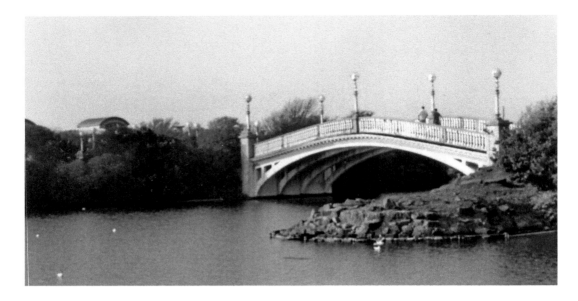

The Venetian Bridge and Walkway

After the First World War, the 1920s saw many changes to the west side of the marine lake, with the consolidation of the area. A stretch of water formed while drainage work was ongoing during land reclamation. This 'lagoon', as it was referred to, was finally drained and landscaped to form today's Prince's Park, opened by the Prince of Wales (later Edward VII) in 1921. The new Pleasureland opened in the period 1920–22. The completion of Prince's Park led to the building of the Colonnade open-air theatre and a new circular swimming pool in 1928. In view of these additional attractions, plus racing car competitions on the beach, better access was required towards Prince's Park. This new access was via a 'Venetian Bridge' across the lake, opened in 1931. The bridge is shown here in the 1950s and in 2012, looking at the bridge and islands from the south side.

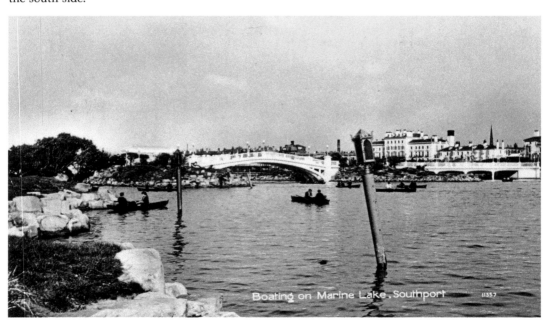

Boating on Marine Lake, Southport   11357

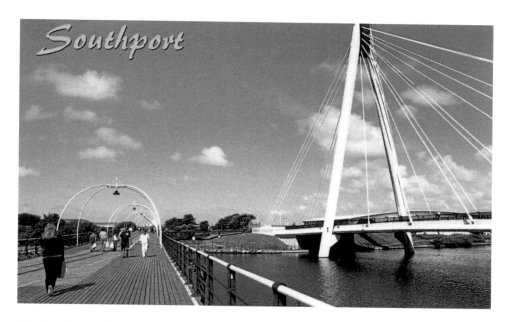

Marine Way Bridge

The original Marine Drive/Way with its bridge over the lake was opened in 1895, the same year that the north and south lakes were joined together close to the bridge. The old postcard view looks over the bridge to the beach. To the right is the bridge itself, supported on iron columns. Above the bridge the outline of the first sea bathing lake is visible. It was superseded in 1928 when the circular pool was built in Prince's Park. The buildings were at 'Peter Pan's Playground' (which included the bathing lake). To the left is the pier, which closed in 1997 due to its poor condition. Refurbished and rebuilt, it reopened in 2002. The old Marine Way Bridge was also demolished between 2002 and 2004 due to its poor condition, and the new suspension bridge was built and opened in 2004. The new bridge and pier are shown in today's postcard image.

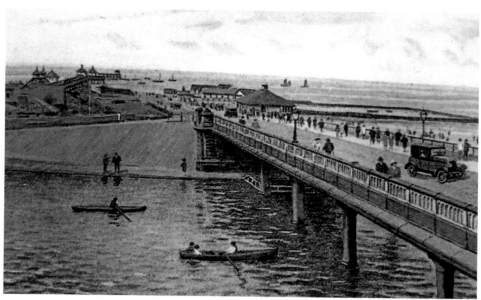

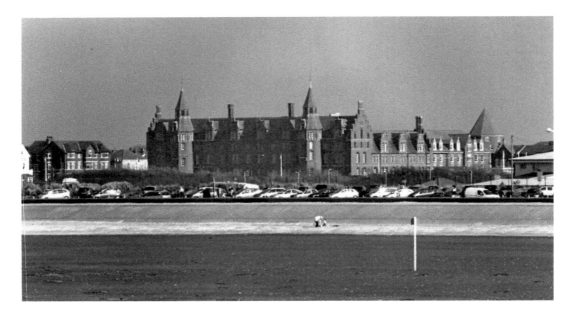

The North Marine Lake

Recession of the sea from Southport's beaches had been compensated for by the creation of a marine lake south of the pier in 1887. The lake became a major attraction and a north lake was proposed in around 1890. It would run northwards from the north side of the pier, alongside the promenade, to approximately where Albany Road is today. To the seaward side of the lake, high tides overran the embankment enclosing the lake area and were a great attraction for visitors to watch. The lake was completed and opened in 1892, along with some garden areas at the promenade side of the lake. The old view was taken from approximately the beach end of Marine Way, looking back to the promenade and the former hospital. Today's image looks across the beach, north ocean Plaza and north marine lake, now some way from the sea.

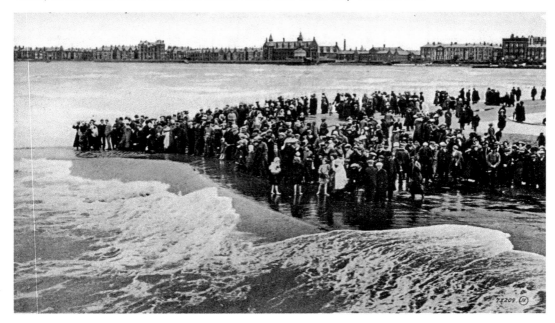

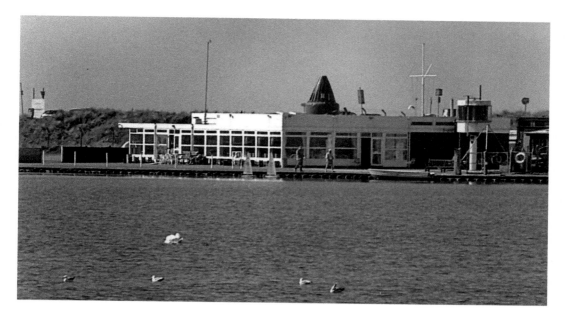

Lakeside Consolidation

To consolidate the west bank of the north lake, where a new Marine Drive and bridge were being built, a stone embankment was laid. It is believed this photograph dates from 1895 and shows work the progress of work to join the north and south lakes by removing a sandbank between them (right of centre). The elongation of the west side bank of the lake, on which men are standing, appears to be underway, advancing northwards to eventually enclose the lake. Note the three-masted sailing ship moored approximately where today the west bank of the lake is located, and where Southport's Yacht and Sailing Clubhouse and moorings are to be found – shown in today's view, which looks across the lake from the promenade. The lake was widened when two islands were created in 1963, and extended northwards again in 1966.

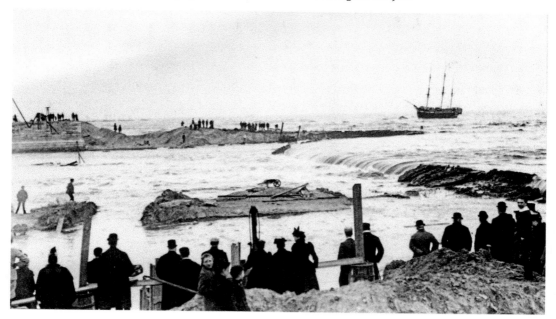

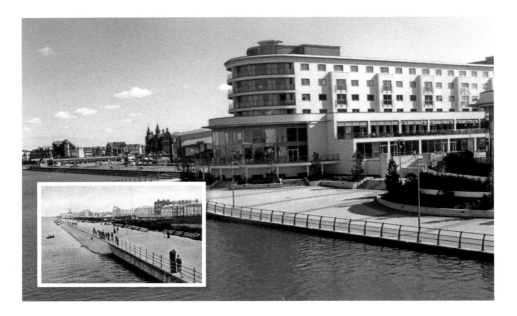

North Lake Gardens

The promenade side of the lake was built with a wide footpath to lakeside railings with views over the lake to the west. Between this footpath and promenade road was a garden area called Marine Gardens, featuring lawns and floral displays. The promenade road at this time was raised, with bridges below it giving access to roads running down to Lord Street. In the old inset view one such bridge is visible near to the 1866-built Queens Hotel. In the gardens close to the pier was a bandstand with a large area for spectators attending concert presentations. in 1930 a new conference centre was built, covering part of the gardens, though the bandstand and spectator area were retained. It was renamed the Floral Hall in 1932 and is shown in our 1960s image. Today the new Ramada Hotel complex covers the former gardens

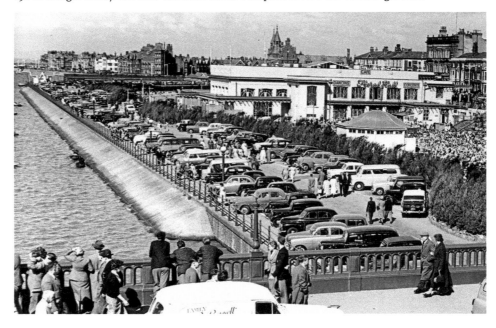

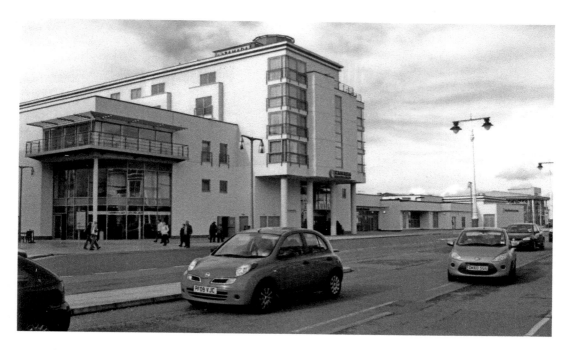

Floral Hall and Gardens

Here again we see the Floral Hall in all its wonderful simplicity, with gardens that were such a pleasant place in which to watch concerts. They were much more aesthetically attractive before the addition of the new theatre and later the conference centre. Note the north lake (above the hall), before its widening in 1963. The theatre was created due to the loss of the Garrick and other venues in the town. It was opened in May 1973 by no less a famous personality than Marlene Dietrich, film star and singer – though it was due to be carried out by Morecambe and Wise! Today, part of the original Floral Hall is visible on the lakeside. The hall and theatre were refurbished in 2007/08. Of the gardens, sadly nothing remains. In 2008 they were built over by the Ramada Hotel complex; its frontage is shown above. It does not do for the area what the gardens used to do!

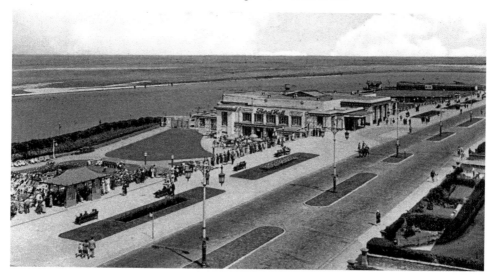

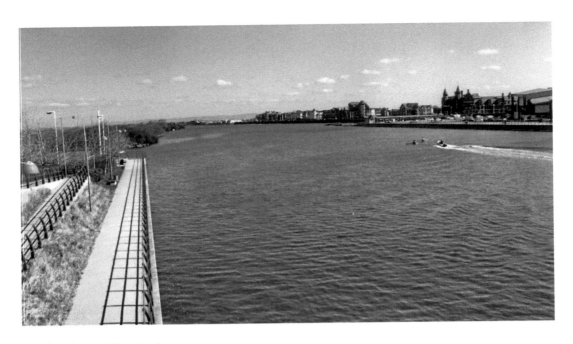

North Lake Paddling Pool

About 1910 an area within the west side of north lake immediately adjoining the Marine Drive Bridge was fenced off and made shallower by sand depositions to a depth of just a few inches only, for a children's paddling pool. There is much of interest in the photograph. Firstly, the line of the original lake width is visible to the top left. Also, a windmill can be seen very clearly across the lake at the promenade side. This was sited on top of the building where today the Smallest Pub is located, across from the former hospital. The windmill drove a water pump, which drew water from the lake to fill water carts to clean Southport's streets. In today's view of the lake we look to the north end. The islands created in the 1963 widening are to the left.

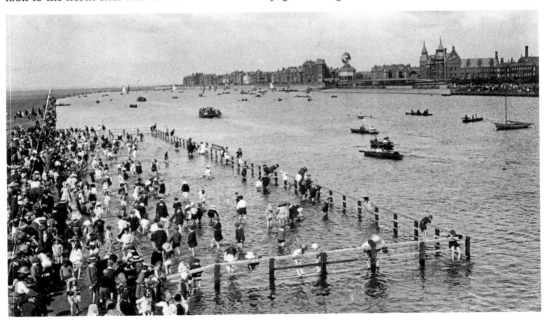

68

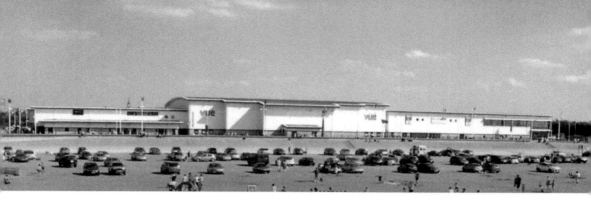

Beach Car Park

When I was loaned this aerial image showing the beach and cars on it, the first thing I did was to see if my own car was there, for during the 1960s I visited this area frequently. I didn't find my car. The image is so nostalgic, for if not the beach there was the open-air swimming pool, the fair at Pleasureland, the pier or Prince's Park for picnics and ball games. I was unable to obtain a modern view of this location, but felt the image was of great interest to regular Southport visitors like me. Today, the open-air pool has been replaced (why was the old building not covered with a dome?) by a hotel, cinema, and commercial units, as part of south Ocean Plaza development. In the 'today' view we look across the beach past parked cars to the frontage of the new Vue cinema complex.

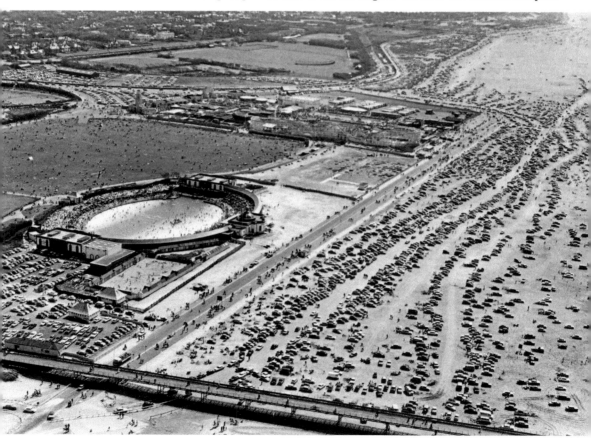

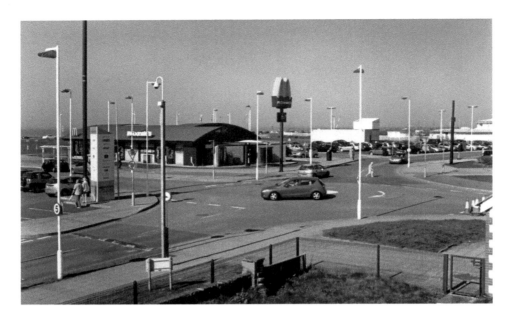

Peter Pan's Playground

Located to the north side of the Marine Way, and close to the beach, this location was of prime interest for young children (and parents), from the later 1920s into the 1960s or possibly '70s. It was a place where one would not have to pay out large amounts of money for amusements, but above all one's children were in a safe environment. A little way up the road there was also the visitors' day nursery where young children could be left for a time, so that parents could have 'a bit of peace and quiet'! Within the complex the large open-air swimming pool had been incorporated and made shallower to cater for young children as well. The site entrance location is about where one turns into the new north Ocean Plaza development off Marine Way today, just about where McDonald's restaurant is found. The 2012 view was taken from the pier.

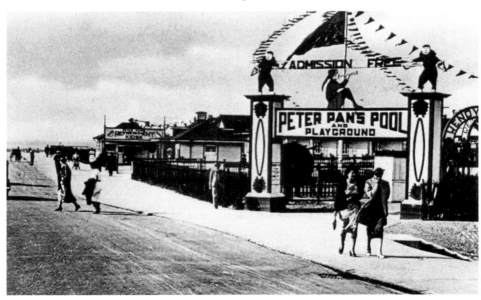

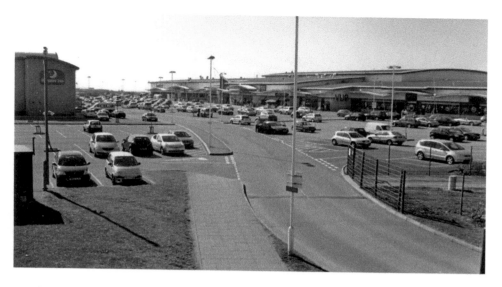

South Ocean Plaza

Today, also viewed from the pier, we look at the site once occupied by the circular open-air bathing pool. Immediately in the foreground is the entrance to a car park between buildings to the left and right. On the left is a large hotel. To the right, is a Vue cinema. Each side are numerous commercial outlets and gymnasia. The whole of the Ocean Plaza redevelopment of the foreshore has met with many stumbling blocks along the way. There was even debate as to whether such a venture should have been built here or not; as they say, 'the jury is still out', but the complex is up and running now anyway. I use the swimming pool itself for my old image, once again rekindling many happy memories of time spent at this location, where now there is the cinema and car park.

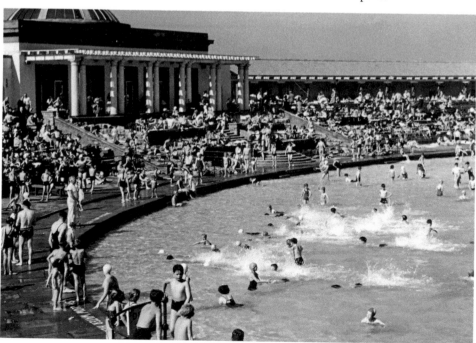

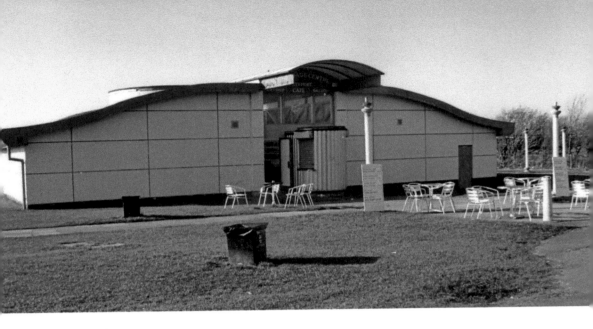

The Colonnade

The access to Prince's Park from the promenade was improved after 1931 when the bridge was opened crossing the south marine lake. A path from the bridge ran towards the open-air swimming pool. Across this path was built a horseshoe-shaped building in plan, in which an open-air theatre was created. Around the sides of the 'horseshoe' was a covered, colonnaded walkway, which provided some shelter from the wind. A small stage was set at the closed end of the 'shoe', as can be seen from the old image here. Popular into the 1960s, it succumbed to change. It was closed for a time and was reopened after alterations as a skating rink. Eventually reduction in usage again led to its demise, to reopen again in the 1980s. Today the new building hosts an interesting collection of enlarged old postcard illustrations around the walls of a café.

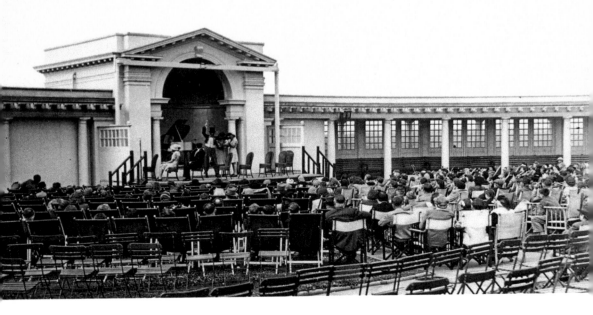

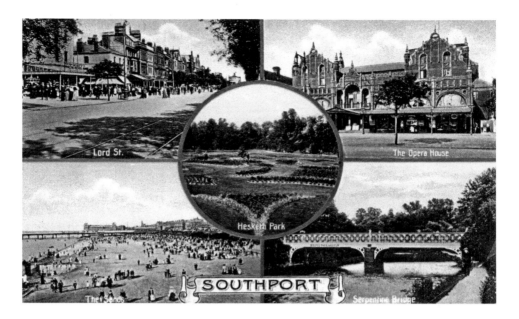

A Postcard From Southport

The postcards that we love to choose for friends and relatives while we are at the seaside have been around from the early 1900s. The earliest I personally have was posted in Southport and dates from 1904, for which I recently paid £3. Since then, how many thousands of Southport images have travelled around the country and still do? I thought, as we near the end of our nostalgic look back, how things used to be and how they have changed 'through time'. The card I selected was posted in March 1912 and has five different general views of Southport. Today's image is a card currently on sale in the town and has four modern pictures: Lord Street, Pier entrance, Pier deck and the Theatre (formerly Floral Hall) – oh yes, and 'Greetings From Southport'.

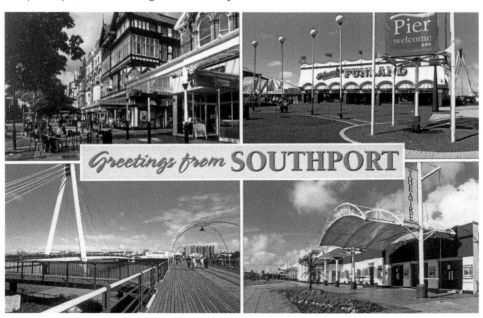

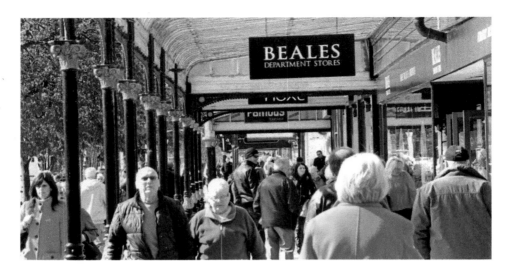

Lord Street Shoppers

As we have seen previously, Southport's Lord Street is a place to browse, have a coffee at a pavement café, visit the wide variety of shops, or just sit and 'peole watch'. My final view of the street shows a typical morning parade of shoppers, in May 2012, under the shopfront canopies that are a major feature of the boulevard.

Acknowledgements

I would like to acknowledge the help and co-operation of the following organisations and individuals in the research and compilation of *Southport Through Time*.

Firstly, the many authors, past and present, whose works I have read and digested for their views and historical interpretations, gleanings and anecdotes which I now 'interpret' for *Southport Through Time*. Secondly, the manufacturers, both national and local, of many old postcard images of the town from the 1900s to 2012.

Staff and employees of the Metropolitan Borough of Sefton; the Department of Tourism and Leisure; the *Southport Visiter* staff and archives. Staff of Churchtown Library Staff, Chapel Street Railway Station and the Lakeside Miniature Railway. Staff at numerous shops and stores in Lord Street, Chapel Street, Wayfarer's Arcade, Cambridge Arcade and Royal Arcade. Morrison's supermarket and members of staff at the retail outlets at the North and South Ocean Plaza complex.

Additionally: M. Duffy, Mrs D. Firgarth, Mrs G. Scott, Mrs D. Nateby, G. Isaacs, R. Percival, A. Gibbons, H. Soden. And friends: Jim and Pat Monks, Barry and Teresa Holden, Bob and Pat Catterall, Margaret Rawlings, Wilma Gregory, and Wilf & Norma Culshaw, now in Lisbon, Portugal, for their continuing support and encouragement. Finally, to my partner Barbara Morgan, for her patience, computer skills and 'recommendations'!

A big thank you to all concerned.

Jack Smith